1850 *to* 1920

LOOKING BACK

*A pictorial view of the
Lehigh Valley and
surrounding counties*

Published by

THE
MORNING
CALL

The Morning Call gratefully acknowledges

the following individuals and organizations for their contributions of photographs and

research support: Matthew Brown, Robert Bungerz, Edith Freed, Carol Front, Bill Harr,

Tom Heard, Raymond E. Holland Regional and Industrial History Collection,

George and Grace Knapp, Glenn Koch, Lehigh County Historical Society, Lance Metz,

Muhlenberg College, National Canal Museum, Perkasie Historical Society,

Quakertown Historical Society, Vic Stahl, John Stoudt.

Researcher/author: Frank Whelan

Editor: Alice J. Lesoravage

Design Editor: Jeffery Lindenmuth

Photo Editor: Denis McElroy

New Products Director: Lisa Bergus

Project Coordinators: Mary Youtz, Sara Mercer

Staff: Ellison Beers, Kim Christman, Ron Culver, Betty Frack, Tim Frankenfield, Shelly Gould, Elaine Hall, Sally Jo Lawrence, Andrea Lesko, Keith Lewis, Barbara Curmaci Mathews, Catherine Meredith, Martha Miller, Eva Ng, Larry Printz, Paul Strisovsky, Ann Vanic, Jane White, Kathy Williamson.

 Cover photo: Dedication of the Soldiers and Sailors Monument in Allentown's Center Square, Oct. 19, 1899.

Published by The Morning Call
101 North Sixth Street
P.O. Box 1260
Allentown, PA 18105-1260

Library of Congress
Catalog Card Number:
98-66246

ISBN 0-9664197-0-7
Printed in the USA
1998

INDEX

ALLENTOWN

Early on Oct. 15, 1862, Allentown photographer Benjamin Lochman positioned a camera to shoot out the window of his studio at 9 W. Hamilton St., just off Center Square.

A light, wet snow from the night before clung to roofs and awnings and rested gently on Breinig & Leh's Lion Hall, the ancestor of what would be Leh's department store. Sleigh tracks and pedestrian paths were evident, but not a soul was visible in the street.

Lochman pressed the shutter release and took the first known dated view of the city.

Zion Reformed Church's colonial-style steeple rises to the right in the photograph. A sign for the Eagle Hotel is in the left foreground. A row of two-and three-story businesses lines the south side of Hamilton Street. In the distance, the outline of South Mountain is visible.

No one knows for certain when the first professional photographer came to Allentown, but by 1860, the first city directory lists three photographers under the category "Daguerreotypes and Photographs."

Some 135 years and several million photographs later, Allentown has undergone many changes.

This chapter covers the period from the 1850s to the 1920s. It shows the transformation of a largely Pennsylvania-German farming community into an industrial city that produced everything from silk to typewriters.

This is a visual history of that change and the people who made it happen.

Hamilton Street, just off Center Square, looking east, taken in 1862 by Allentown photographer Benjamin Lochman.

When the U.S. Army Ambulance Service Corps was stationed at Camp Crane at the Allentown Fairgrounds from 1917 to 1919, its ambulance was used for advertising.

The Camp Crane Band was a popular group in Allentown during World War I. The band could be counted upon to add music to any patriotic event. The camp based at the Allentown Fairgrounds was named for Charles Henry Crane, U.S. Army Surgeon General 1882-83. It was a training ground for the Army Ambulance Corps. The federal government leased the fairgrounds from the Lehigh County Agricultural Society from May 24, 1917 to April 9, 1919 for the camp.

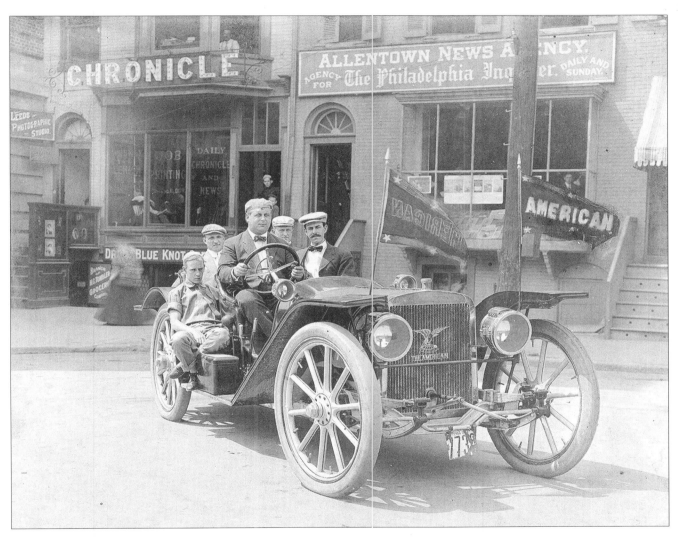

The Iredell family, among Allentown's leaders at the turn of the century, owned the Allentown Chronicle and News from 1870 to 1915. In this 1909 photo in Allentown's Center Square, Robert Iredell is at the wheel of a car known as an American. The Chronicle office is in the background. The man in mechanic's clothes (left) is Lloyd Iredell, who worked on cars as a hobby. In 1911, at age 31, he was killed not far from this spot by the blade of a propeller-driven experimental car.

As the result of a sudden thaw on Feb. 28, 1902, flood waters came charging down the Lehigh River toward Allentown. This picture shows the Hamilton Street bridge looking east. Later, the water smashed the bridge, carrying off the two sections visible in the photo. The bridge was replaced with a temporary span months later, and years later a permanent bridge was built.

The 1902 flood washed into Allentown's industrial district along the Lehigh and Little Lehigh creek. The next day crowds went out to survey the damage, including derailed Lehigh Valley Railroad box cars.

Rising water in the industrial area of Allentown is evident in this 1902 photo by S.W. Ochs. Perhaps the Cubanola advertised on the building in the foreground was a brand of cigar.

The John L. Trexler limekiln in East Allentown was one of Allentown's many industries in the late 1800s. The Hanover Acres housing project occupies part of the site today.

Dorney Park, founded in 1860 as a country hotel, was a popular place at the turn of the century. By 1910, it had developed into a small amusement center with the slogan, "The Natural Spot." Rowing on Dorney Park Lake was a good way to catch a passing breeze on a hot summer afternoon. Cedarbrook County Home and the trolley line of the Allentown & Reading Traction Co. are seen (at right) in the background.

The groundbreaking for Allentown's underground comfort station took place just off the southeast corner of Center Square on Sept. 16, 1919. Wielding the hammer is John "Jack" Allen, a city councilman and prominent 6th Ward resident. In light-colored fedora is City Engineer Harry F. Bascom who designed the station. The contractor George F. Hardner is to his right. The facility included toilets, sinks, a shoeshine stand and a cigar stand.

This Aug. 19, 1919 picture of Hamilton Street, east of 6th Street, is a reminder that actual horse power once moved the city. The event may have been a part of a work-horse parade, planned by local merchants to show off their teams.

The staff at the Hamilton Grocery Co., 1049 Hamilton St., promised a variety of goods as shown in this picture taken in 1905.

There weren't many buildings in the 1000 block of S. 8th Street when this picture was taken in 1916. According to information on the back of the picture, these houses are at 1020 and 1022 S. 8th Street. City directories list the first occupants of 1022 as Charles B. Korn, a draftsman, and wife Mame. There is no listing for 1020.

This distinctive building at 209 N. 7th St. in Allentown was built in 1896 as the home of Thomas E. Ritter, his wife, Mary, and children Lloyd, Wilmer and Jeanette. Ritter was president of the Second National Bank, a director of Merchants Bank, a city councilman and real estate developer. Small cement steps on the edge of the sidewalk were used to help people getting in and out of carriages. The building was later converted to offices and apartments.

On March 8, 1916, a wet snow fell briefly over Allentown. City Engineer Harry F. Bascom's children, W. Broughton, Franklin B. and James M. and their friends saw an opportunity to throw snowballs and do some shoveling at 1342 Walnut St.

The Leh family was one of Allentown's leading merchant families from the 1850s to the 1990s. This photo was taken on the 79th birthday of store founder Henry Leh on June 24, 1909, at the family's 1533 Hamilton St. home known as "Fountain Heights." Figures on horseback are (from left) Henry Leh's son, George; Henry Leh Sr.; George's son, Henry, and George's brother, John.

An unidentified woman takes a stroll on Franklin Street shortly after it was constructed in the 1890s. This type of row housing was popular in Allentown between 1880 and 1910.

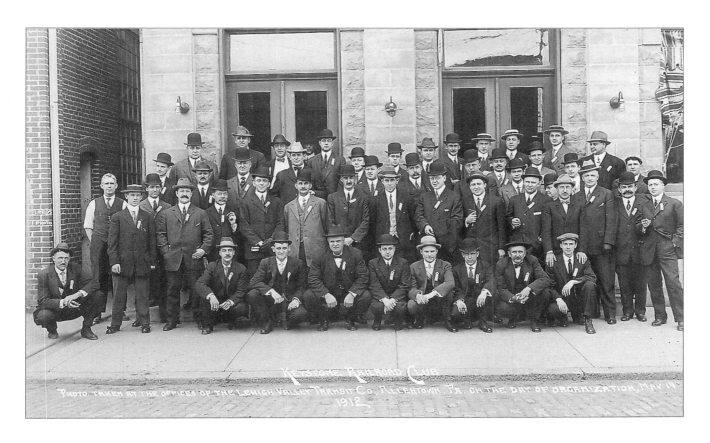

ABOVE
Railroads and street car lines have always had fans in the Lehigh Valley. Members of the Keystone Railroad Club pose outside the Lehigh Valley Transit Co. office at 402-407 N. 14th St. in Allentown on the date of the club's organization, May 14, 1912.

LEFT
Open trolley cars were a popular way to get around on hot summer nights in the early 1900s. This car served the city's 6th Ward.

RIGHT

Allentown's decorative light standards, custom-made by a Canton, Ohio, company and installed in the city in 1916, were called "the hanging gardens of Allentown." They were inspired by flower lamp posts in Europe seen by Maude Reichenbach, wife of then Allentown Mayor Alfred L. "Al" Reichenbach. This one stood in front of the J.A. Wuchter Music Co. at 927 Hamilton St.

BELOW

W.H. Appel's Jewelry store was one of many in Allentown that prided itself on fancy window displays. This one was at 619 Hamilton St. for Christmas 1895.

ABOVE

Grocer George S. Trump was one of many proprietors of small businesses, which were the backbone of Allentown at the turn of the century. This 1900s picture shows Trump and his wife, Alice, in front of their store at 826 S. 7th St. The Trumps lived above the store.

LEFT

One of the best known political figures in early 20th century Allentown was Fred Lewis. A progressive Republican, Lewis was the city's mayor for three terms, 1896-99, 1902-05 and 1932-36. In the late 1940s, Lewis wrote a history column for The Morning Call. Lewis bore a striking resemblance to his hero, Theodore Roosevelt, which he often played up by wearing "Teddy"-style pince-nez eye glasses.

This photograph of the corner of 4th and Turner streets in Allentown, taken in 1916, shows that street repairs are nothing new.

When London, England, native Alfred Clare built this home — a bungalow-style in an era of Queen Anne architecture and row houses — at 29 S. 13th St. in 1904-05, Allentown residents had never seen anything quite like it. The distinctive structure was purchased a few years later by prominent businessman A. Edwin Barber, pictured here with his family. The exterior of the house remains virtually unchanged today.

LEFT
The Rialto in the 900 block of Hamilton Street was among the best known movie theaters in Allentown. It was built in 1917 to replace the Lyceum Theater that burned in 1916. On Dec. 16, 1927, the city's first talking film, "The Prince of Headwaiters" starring Lewis Stone, best remembered as Judge Hardy, the movie father of Mickey Rooney in the Andy Hardy film series, was shown at the Rialto.

BELOW
This view of S. 4th Street, circa 1900, shows the Lehigh Valley Railroad Station with its turrets in the background. Built in 1890 on stone piers over the Jordan Creek, the station was torn down in the 1960s. The large house was probably No. 11, a boarding house run by Anna Knauss.

This view of E. Hamilton Street around 1918 is looking west toward the old Hamilton Street Bridge. The ribbons of steel rails and overhead wires are a reminder of the extensive trolley system that once tied the Lehigh Valley communities together.

This rare photo shows the interior of the Central of New Jersey and Philadelphia and Reading Railroad's freight station at Race and Linden streets around 1890. Note the horseshoe and picture of a ship on the office wall.

The Palace Pharmacy at 602 Hamilton St. featured a soda fountain in all its glory. This picture, taken about 1904, shows that children were provided with a small table and chairs for their treats.

World War I was a time of patriotism in the Lehigh Valley. This picture shows members of the Daughters of the American Revolution on April 8, 1918, at Trout Hall sewing items for soldiers. The DAR also helped with the restoration of Trout Hall.

ABOVE
The Allen Fire Company No. 7, formed in 1871, was popular both as a fire-fighting organization and a social group. The company was based at 2nd and Hamilton streets and later moved to Ridge Avenue. After 1902, it moved to 136 Linden St. This picture was taken in the 1870s.

RIGHT
With a ladder attached to the wagon, the men of Fearless Fire Company of South Allentown look ready for any emergency in this 1900-era winter photograph. At the time South Allentown was a separate borough.

This photo taken in Allentown's Center Square shows a classic steam pumper fire engine at the turn of the century. They were introduced into Allentown in 1865 but were replaced by gasoline-powered fire trucks in the 1920s.

Koch & Person was one of many men's clothing stores that served the city at the turn of the century. This photo shows the store at its original location at 634 Hamilton St.

At the turn of the century, Kramer's Music Store at 544 Hamilton Street was a popular place for sheet music, instruments and busts of great composers. According to a family story, as a young man, Frederick Kramer Sr. wanted to become a musical director of an opera company and had even signed a contract. But his mother thought a stage career was immoral and she ripped up the contract and forbade him to pursue the career. So, he began a music business that his family operated until 1962.

This photograph of the office in the Lafayette Hotel at 133-137 N. 7th St. was taken about 1910. At that time, the hotel was best known for the many traveling salesmen who were guests. The Lafayette was destroyed in one of the city's worst fires on a bitterly cold night, Jan. 23, 1926. Thirteen people were killed and 39 injured.

The Fountain House Hotel, built in 1867, was at the southwest corner of Jefferson and Lawrence streets. It was popular in the 1870s and 1880s as a summer resort, especially for New York theater and opera people who enjoyed tree-covered paths and the water of Crystal Spring. By 1887, the failing resort was acquired by the city as part of its waterworks. Much reduced in size, the building was converted to a tool shed and then removed in the 1960s when Lawrence Street, now Martin Luther King Jr. Drive, was widened.

American House, Allentown, Pa.

The American House Hotel at the northeast corner of 6th and Hamilton streets was a popular place for visitors to Allentown from the late 19th to the early 20th centuries. It was owned by the Seagreaves family, who operated a hotel or inn on that site from the 1850s. The American House was torn down in 1925-26 and replaced by the Americus, now Clarion Hotel, which still occupies the site.

The Hotel Allen, built in 1886 at the northeast corner of 7th and Hamilton streets, quickly became the city's most popular hotel. Presidents Theodore Roosevelt and William Howard Taft were among the notables who lodged there. This rare interior photo shows the lobby in its Edwardian splendor. The Allen was torn down in the early 1950s to make way for First National Bank.

The Manhattan Hotel, which began as the Rittersville Hotel, was at Club and Hanover avenues in Allentown, across from the entrance to Central Park amusement center. When this picture was taken in the 1880s, the building was owned by the Ritter family, who had founded the surrounding community known as Rittersville. Behind the hotel, to the left, was a racetrack that later became the Manhattan Ball Park, where the Allentown Baseball Club under the management of baseball great Mike "King" Kelly played in 1894. The hotel burned in 1898 when a monkey, kept as a pet by the hotel owner started a fire. The building was replaced by another Manhattan Hotel that was torn down in 1921 to make room for the Manhattan Auditorium, later known as the Empire Ballroom.

The Mountainville Hotel, then located in Salisbury Township, now Allentown, was a popular eating and drinking spot in the Lehigh Valley in the 19th century. This picture dates from the 1880s when the innkeeper was Morton T. Person. He owned the hotel, built in 1856, from 1877 to 1911. In December 1958 this 102-year-old building was destroyed in a huge gas explosion that killed seven people. A modern structure now occupies the site.

BETHLEHEM

Founded in 1741 by the Moravian Church as a religious mission to native Americans, Bethlehem saw some of its most dramatic changes more than 100 years later. In the 1850s, The Lehigh Zinc Co., the Lehigh Valley Railroad and Bethlehem Iron, later Steel Co., all were established in South Bethlehem.

With the steel mills came the photographers. In 1860, H.P. Osborne Sr. advertised in the Bethlehem Directory his "Excelsior Gallery of Photography." Located at "No. 9 opposite Broad Street," it offered "all the requisite advantages for making first class specimens of this beautiful art."

Rapid change in the late 19th and early 20th century transformed both Bethlehem and photography.

In 1917, at the urging of Bethlehem Steel Corp. Chairman Charles M. Schwab, North Bethlehem, the old Moravian town, South Bethlehem, West Bethlehem and Northampton Heights were merged to create the modern city of Bethlehem.

This political change reflected the reality of the links that joined the ethnically diverse, economic powerhouse that the city had become.

By 1920, Bethlehem Steel had its own staff of photographers who were recording the company's rise to preeminence as one of the leading steel makers of the world.

A wooden replica of the giant steam-powered 125-ton steel hammer used by the Bethlehem Iron, later Steel Co., to forge armor plate for the U.S. Navy was displayed at the 1893 World's Fair in Chicago. Steelmaker John Fritz had a steel hammer built at the steel company, based on a similar device he had seen in France. All of South Bethlehem was said to shake when the hammer was in operation.

RIGHT

The 300 block of 3rd Street where Taylor Street intersects, was a busy part of South Bethlehem at the turn of the century. The building on the corner was Frank McGovern's hotel. His home was next door at 302. The building next to his home was Mrs. M. L. McGovern's undertaking establishment.

BELOW

The other side of the 300 block of 3rd Street began with 301, Dr. Rose Barre Sheridan's Pharmacy. Next door is the Lynch Shoe Co. The next two buildings identify the era. The first is a small restaurant called the Verdun Lunch after the great French battle of World War I. Above it is a sign with a painted stars and stripes and the French tri-color. Next door, a storefront offers a chance to buy Liberty Bonds in installments of $1.50. The large building with the two chimneys is the American Hotel run by George Zboyovsky.

LEFT
This view of Broad Street looking west from High shows the part of the city sometimes called North Bethlehem before the merger of 1917. It was primarily a residential middle-class neighborhood of Victorian homes.

BELOW
A view of W. Broad Street in the 1920s shows a tall sign for the Kurtz Restaurant and Cafe at 32 W. Broad St.

The dwelling at left at 250 E. Market St., Bethlehem, belonged to George A. Chandler, a civil engineer and nephew of Bethlehem Steel executive John Fritz. He worked for Bethlehem Steel for 30 years. Chandler was a councilman for North Bethlehem Borough before it was incorporated into the city in 1917. He and his wife, Florence, parents of four children, had a collection of 2,000 books devoted to local history. Man in photo is unidentified.

Downtown Bethlehem in the 1920s bustled with traffic. This picture of Main Street at Broad Street shows the Hotel Bethlehem in the distance. Solomon R. Bush and James V. Bull's Bush & Bull's department store, later Orr's, is visible at right. The sign at left advertised the Sun Inn.

Bernhard Cohen operated a jewelry store at 509 3rd St. on Bethlehem's South Side. Nathan Shapiro's White Star barber shop was at 511. Next door was Gatanis Brothers Grocery, followed by the clothing store of J.M. Silberstein. Benjamin Greenberg's clothing store was at 517.

Looking east from New Street down 3rd Street, the most prominent structure at the corner is the O'Reilly Building owned by E. O'Reilly Clothing Co., outfitters for men and boys. According to the 1920 city directory, the building also housed attorney J. A. Moran, Realtor William Sinwell, the Bethlehem Business College and the Knights of Columbus. Across the street at Bill's Cafe, a small sign offers rooms for rent by the day or hour. The building next door had a large sign in Cyrillic, the alphabet used in Russia, Bulgaria and other Slavic countries.

This photo of Bethlehem Steel's Machine Shop No. 2 shows that the company was one of the major weapons makers of World Wars I and II. The cannon in the lower left foreground was made for the Navy.

Types of wheels made by
Bethlehem Steel were displayed
for customers in exhibit space
No. 2.

Steel wheels were one of
the company's most
popular items. They
were used for trucks and
military vehicles.

ABOVE
These officials are standing on a gun turret for the battleship USS Pennsylvania. Along with its sister ship, the USS Arizona, later destroyed at Pearl Harbor, it was an important part of the U.S. Navy during World War I.

LEFT
Bethlehem Steel's Buffington Crozier disappearing gun, shown in 1898, was used primarily for harbor defenses. It dropped low after firing and could be loaded quickly. Buffington Croziers were part of the defense network of Manila Bay and Pearl Harbor, but as powerful as they were against naval attacks, these guns were of little use against airplanes.

This hydraulic forging press in the Drop Forge Department is making a brake drum for a 5-ton Mack truck, probably an AC Bulldog. Later, during World War II, more than 70 percent of the engine cylinders used in U.S. military planes were made by the Drop Forge Department.

The foundry's small casting division made parts used by Bethlehem Steel for its own machinery.

A trestle for unloading material in stock bins at the Bethlehem Steel blast furnaces carried the largest trolley freight cars in the world on one track and regular gauge railroad cars on another. The building in the background is No. 2 Machine Shop, then the largest enclosed industrial space in the world.

Piles of wood outside Machine Shop No. 6, carpenter-pattern-mechanical-electrical departments, give some idea of the amount of material used by the company. The office building to the right is Bethlehem Steel's former corporate headquarters.

When Bethlehem Steel President Charles Schwab felt he could no longer control the workers at Bethlehem Steel during the strike of 1910, he brought in the State Police, known as the Cossacks, to put down the labor action. Here, the State Police line up for inspection in front of Bethlehem Steel's headquarters.

Mounted members of the State Police are shown taking action against steel workers. One worker was killed and another severely injured by the police before the strike was over.

LEFT
This photo shows mechanics in Bethlehem Steel's No. 3 machine shop in 1907. In 1910, the No. 3 machine shop was in the forefront of the steel strike that shut down the company for 108 days. It was the first major job action at Bethlehem Steel.

BELOW
The creation of steel rails at Lehigh Mills was a dangerous job at Bethlehem Steel. A careless worker could be burned by white-hot steel.

Rail cars are lined up in the stockyard of the open hearth No. 2 Saucon Plant. This plant was built in 1909-1910 to make steel for the new Gray Mill that made wide-flanged beams for skyscrapers.

To give clients a view of the many things Bethlehem Steel produced, the company had several permanent exhibits. Space No. 3 displayed a variety of artillery shells. A sign above describes pipe being made by Bethlehem Steel for the Hudson River Vehicular Tunnel, later known as the Holland Tunnel.

At the turn of the century, Schneller and Snyder, merchant tailors, employed members of the Herlikofer family. This photo shows the Herlikofer family at a company outing.

Opening a hole to tap an open-hearth furnace was among the most dangerous jobs at Bethlehem Steel. The process required workers to insert an iron bar over a bathtub-sized vessel filled with molten metal and pierce a clay plug on the other side to let the liquid metal flow slowly out into a mold.

This view from the west shows Bethlehem Steel blast furnaces built between 1914 and 1920. The tracks are owned by Lehigh Valley Railroad and the building at right was built in 1872 by steelmaker John Fritz.

The first hook and ladder is delivered to Lehigh Hook and Ladder in South Bethlehem in August 1886. Note the leather water buckets underneath.

The first carriage in service for the South Bethlehem Fire Department was acquired in 1876. It was built in 1841 for the Schuylkill Hose Company of Philadelphia.

Martin V. Snyder, a contractor and builder, also sold real estate. Shown is his newly completed home and office at 921 W. Broad St. in Bethlehem about 1910.

Workers and their families from Bethlehem's Bee Hive Store on Main Street enjoy a company picnic.

Martin V. Snyder's grocery store in Bethlehem as it looked in 1915. Note the sign for Jell-O in window.

This picture of a magnificent steam locomotive No. 411, shown in a South Bethlehem railyard, was taken on Aug. 1, 1886. The staff are, in no particular order, conductor James Allen Oldham, assistant engineer Thomas J. Sands, engineer George Green, trainman John Henk, baggage master U.D. Couster and brakemen N.W. Brounie and George Gilbert.

Northampton Heights Hotel, in the borough of Northampton Heights that became a part of Bethlehem after 1917, offered refuge for man and beast in 1895. Proprietor H.F. Beidelman and family stand out front.

Keeping cool in the summer 100 years ago required the ice man. The Artificial Ice Co. at 2nd and New streets in South Bethlehem offered horse-drawn service to your door.

In 1910, people shopped for food and dry goods at corner grocery stores like this one at 702 Wyandotte St.

EASTON

Easton was born of its location at the confluence of the Lehigh and Delaware rivers.

In 1752, it was designated the county seat of Northampton County, which then covered an area between Bucks County and the New York border. Easton's founder, Thomas Penn, son of William Penn, hoped the county seat would become a major center for river trade. But Penn's hopes were dashed when the rivers proved too shallow for most river traffic.

It was not until the creation of the Lehigh and Delaware canals in the 1820s that the water of the normally shallow rivers could be used for commerce. Industry sprung up along the banks of the Lehigh Canal to take advantage of its cheap supply of water power.

By 1860, Easton was the largest town in the Lehigh Valley. It was home to three professional photographers — Reuben Knecht, J.J. Carey and J.K. Thompson.

The arrival of the railroads in the 1850s ended Easton's canal boom. Although it had plenty of industry, the city was hemmed in by hills and lacked the tracts of undeveloped land that Allentown had in abundance. For most of the 19th and early 20th centuries, Easton depended on the legal business generated by the county courthouse and its role as a regional commercial center.

The arrival of Hugh Moore's Dixie Cup Co. in neighboring Wilson in 1920 added a new industry and a new business leader who would play a significant role in shaping Easton's future.

In June 1886, the arrival in Easton of a fanciful canal boat on the Lehigh and Delaware Canal, carrying socialite artist Louis Comfort Tiffany and friends, sparked a great deal of interest. One spectator in the crowd was this member of the Easton Wheelmen, a cycling club, wearing his riding outfit. His bicycle, known as a high-wheeler, ordinary or penny-farthing, was created in the 1870s. It took real skill to ride it.

ABOVE

In 1897, shoppers at Maxwell's book store on the northeast corner of Easton's Centre Square had this view of the city's green space. Note the "huckster wagons" of farmers who had come to town to sell produce.

LEFT

The Taylor Building on S. 4th Street, also known as the First Ward Schoolhouse, was one of Easton's early public schools. It was named for George Taylor, founding father and the only Lehigh Valley signer of the Declaration of Independence. Built between 1870-1873, the three-story mansard-roofed brownstone cost $96,139.

The Karldon Hotel, on the northwest corner of N. 3rd and Spring Garden streets, opened as the United States Hotel on March 24, 1898. It was torn down in the 1970s and replaced by Valley Federal Savings Bank.

In this view of the homes along N. 3rd Street in 1900, the Karldon Hotel is visible on the left at the far end of the street.

This photo shows Lafayette College's Pardee Hall after a fire on Dec. 18, 1897. Firefighters were plagued by a lack of water pressure on College Hill and the blaze burned for hours. The loss was estimated at $200,000. It was the second fire at the site — the building had burned to the ground on June 24, 1879.

At the turn of the century, Easton's City Hall was moved into this Victorian mansion at 650 Cherry St. It had been the home of Dr. Traill Green, a professor of chemistry at Lafayette College, who donated money to build an observatory at the college. City government was moved from the building in 1936.

The Drake Building at 17-19 S. 3rd St. in 1899 was a magnificent seven-story example of a 19th century office building. Its classic cast-iron facade was one of the finest outside a major city in the country. It was owned by J. Drake's Sons, a wholesale grocery business. The building was torn down in 1972 to make way for a four-story parking garage.

Trolley cars were the major form of urban transit in Easton in the early 20th century. This photo of E. Northampton Street around 1900 shows two trolleys in operation.

Downtown Easton, looking east down Northampton Street, was a bustle of activity at the turn of the century. Judging from the straw hats on the men and the woman holding a parasol, the season is summer and the flags and bunting suggest it may be July 4.

Visitors to Island Park, on Smith Island on the Lehigh River, were offered a number of amusements from 1894 to 1920. Besides sports and picnics, you could impress your friends by getting your own postcard photo taken.

During the summer, 19th century residents of Easton could think of no better place to be than Island Park, which was created by the Easton Transit Co., a local trolley line. From 1894 to 1919, thousands took the trolley to Smith Island on the Lehigh River where they enjoyed a picnic area, a baseball diamond and a building known as The Casino where band leader John Philip Sousa performed. Ice jams destroyed the trolley bridge so many times that the transit company closed the park in 1920.

A popular amusement at Island Park in Easton was this miniature railroad. It operated from 1900 to 1920.

V. R. R. Station, Easton, Pa.

The Lehigh Valley Railroad opened a rail line to Easton on Nov. 27, 1852. This depot, built in the 1880s, was considered one of the most important stations on the line at the time. It was replaced by another station in the 1920s.

In this 1920 photo, a dredge is shown operating on the Lehigh Canal. The Chain Dam across the Lehigh River and the trolley bridge to Island Park are in the background.

This pedestrian suspension bridge built in 1885 linked Warren and Valley streets in Easton. It opened on Aug. 30, 1886 as a toll bridge. Funds to build the structure were raised by selling 1,500 shares of common stock at $20 a share. The bridge, subject to high winds, was damaged severely by storms in 1939 and in November 1950. It was torn down in 1951.

Easton's covered bridge over the Delaware River weathered more then a few floods. This photo shows it in the late 19th century.

Although it's known as the Free Bridge today, in the early 20th century toll takers manned Easton's Northampton Street Bridge. The bridge was built in 1895 by the Delaware Bridge Co., a subsidiary of Easton Transit Co., to replace a covered bridge. In 1921, the newly formed Delaware River Joint Toll Commission abolished the toll.

The covered bridge that spanned the Delaware River at Easton from 1805 to 1895 was built by New England builder Timothy Palmer. It was the only bridge on the river north of Trenton to survive the flood of 1841. It was torn down in 1895 out of fear that a fire could be sparked by the electric trolley lines across it. The Northampton Street Bridge, sometimes called the Free Bridge, was built to replace it.

The white cupola on St. John's Lutheran Church is visible at far left in this photograph of Easton looking north from Mount Ida, the cliff off Route 611 on the south side of the Lehigh River. Mount Ida overlooked the old Lehigh Valley Railroad passenger station and bridge in Easton.

Easton began its life as a waterfront city. This late 19th century picture shows the industries that were built at the confluence of the Lehigh and Delaware rivers and along the Lehigh Canal. The building with a turret roof at left is Jersey Central Railroad Station. Almost every structure visible in this photograph was torn down in the 1960s as part of urban renewal.

RIGHT

The graceful arched entrance to Easton's covered bridge bears the year it was built, 1805, and the name of the builder, T. Palmer. The words under it warn, "Caution. Keep to the Right. All Persons Riding or Driving Over This Bridge Faster Than a Walk Will be Punished as the Law Directs."

BELOW

Glendon was an industrial suburb of Easton founded with money from New England investors. Glendon was under the control of English-born iron master William Firmstone in the 1850s. This photo shows the Glendon covered bridge over the Lehigh River as it looked in the 1890s.

ABOVE
Glendon Iron Works employees are shown in this 1880s photograph. Note the tools in the workers' hands and lack of safety gear.

LEFT
Glendon Iron Works is shown running full force in the 1880s.

LEHIGH

Lehigh County, founded in 1812, owes its birth to Pennsylvania German farmers who had been unhappy for years about having to make the long journey to Easton every time they had to go to court.

Thanks in large measure to the influence of the region's leading citizen, Anne Penn Allen Greenleaf, granddaughter of Allentown founder William Allen, the state legislature agreed to split Lehigh from Northampton County with Allentown as the county seat.

Although the area remained primarily rural with farms and small towns, change was not absent from Lehigh County in the late 19th century. From the 1850s to the 1880s, pig iron furnaces transformed towns like Catasauqua and Hockendauqua into industrial centers. Farming gradually changed and became more mechanized. And although aware of the importance of outside markets, Lehigh County farmers found themselves even more tied to what was happening in far away places like Chicago.

The county's population remained largely Pennsylvania German. They had large families which could not be accommodated on the farm. Many migrated into Allentown, taking leading roles in industry, banking and the law, thus shaping the city's character as a Pennsylvania-German center.

The Civil War drew many Lehigh County men to the great conflict. Among them was William Harrison "Harry" Reitz of New Tripoli. He also participated in the battles of South Mountain, Antietam and Chancellorsville. The picture of Reitz and his wife, Brigitta (Scheetz), was taken at the Gettysburg Battlefield in 1900.

Many rural tradesmen traveled the back roads of Lehigh County in wagons similar to this at the turn of the century. Note the rolled-up cloth shade that when lowered kept the elements and road dust off the driver.

Pearson Snyder, a butcher in New Tripoli, shows off his wagon. The photograph was taken by James Snyder, a well-known local photographer about 1910.

These two New Tripoli women are out for a ride on the dirt roads of Lynn Township at the turn of the century. Their fancy hats suggest that they were off to pay a Sunday call. The unusual looking harness was designed to keep the horseflies from startling the horse.

New Tripoli tradesman butcher Victor N. Metzger poses for photographer James Snyder on July 1, 1911.

Teaching in a one-room schoolhouse was the occupation of Lillie Fritch who was employed at Weaver's School outside of New Tripoli. Among her tasks would have been controlling pupils ages 6 to 15, keeping the room clean and firing the pot-bellied stove on cold winter mornings. Fritch's hat was the height of fashion and her long, immaculate, white skirt suggests long hours spent at the wash tub.

ABOVE
In the iron horse era, the railroad station at Wanamaker, Lynn Township, was the link for many rural communities to the world beyond.

LEFT
Work was not the only thing that kept New Tripoli folks occupied at the turn of the century. This photo shows a number of them camping along the banks of the Ontelaunee Creek. According to information on the back of the photo, the men are (from left) Charles Snyder, Ralph Snyder, Charles Krause and Nathan Weiss and their wives and families.

Potatoes were Lehigh County's main crop at the turn of the century and Lynn Township was the major potato-producing region in the county at the time. Over 2 million bushels were produced in 1912. This photo shows the William Mantz family plowing the potato crop. Their ancestors had settled in the New Tripoli area in 1778.

William Hoffman's farm was one of New Tripoli's largest potato-raising operations. In 1912, he shipped 161,000 bushels or 230 railroad carloads from his 98-acre property. His other interests included a coal and grain dealership. This photo shows some of the farm workers, mostly local families, who helped make those potato crops possible.

Speaker Dr. Thomas L. Montgomery turns toward the crowd during the Muhlenberg Library cornerstone laying ceremony in 1926.

The laying of the cornerstone at Muhlenberg College Library, now Haas Hall Administration building, on May 21, 1926 was an important moment for the school's history. To the left in academic robes is Dr. J.A.W. Haas, college president. At right in cap and gown is Reuben J. Butz, local attorney and president of Muhlenberg College Board of Trustees. In academic robes to left of Butz is Dr. George T. Ettinger, Latin professor and dean of the college. Man in suit holding hat, standing behind Butz, is Dr. Thomas L. Montgomery, librarian of the Pennsylvania Historical Society, the featured speaker of the day. The man in light suit directly behind cornerstone is the Rev. J.C. Rauch who was in charge of construction.

ABOVE

This group of turn-of-the-century Muhlenberg College biology students is shown dissecting frogs. Apparently suits and ties were required wear at the college in those days.

LEFT

This turn-of-the-century Muhlenberg College chemistry class gathers around awaiting the professor's lecture. Apparently exposed pipes in the ceiling were not considered an aesthetic drawback, even in a new building.

 This photo shows 1912 Muhlenberg College students engaged in what looks like a form of aerobics. Some of the students wear canvas shoes, and others are barefoot.

The Muhlenberg gymnasium around 1912 featured the latest in exercise equipment. The gym was the responsibility of Physical Director Willis P. Bachman, in photo above right.

Muhlenberg College's reception room, in the Ettinger Building, in the early 1900s was furnished sparsely. Notice the lighting fixtures that could switch to gas if the electric lights failed.

In the 1920s, the Muhlenberg College band was often called on to provide music for pep rallies and football games. This photo shows the band assembled in front of the library.

This view looking south on 5th Street in Emmaus gives an interesting glimpse of the community at the dawn of the 20th century.

The Emmaus Hotel at 23 S. 5th St. was a welcome sight for travelers on the dirt roads of the 19th century. When this picture was taken around 1910, its innkeeper, William K. Faust, served Neuweiler beer to thirsty travelers. Today the building is the VFW home.

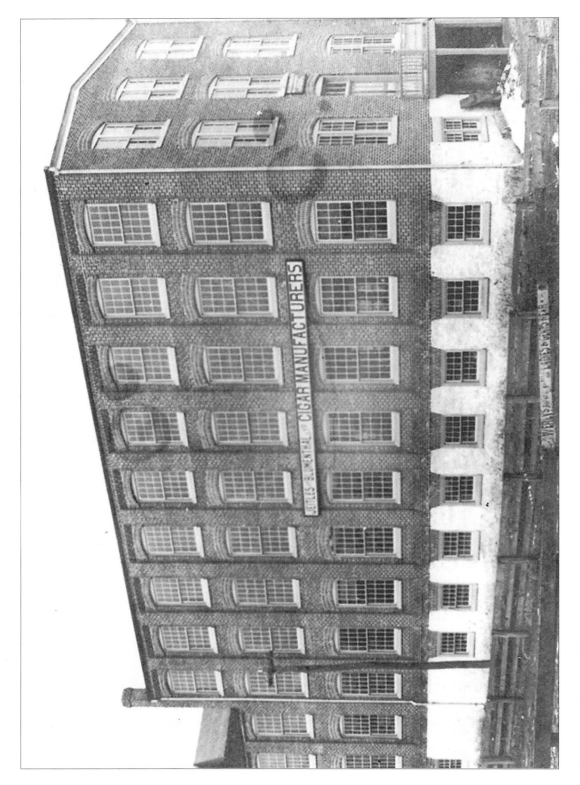

Emmaus was the home of many industries in the early 20th century. In 1905, the Jeitles and Blumenthal Cigar Co. opened this building on 2nd Street. At its height in 1914, the business employed 200 people and turned out between 150 and 170 cigars a day. By the 1930s, the structure had been converted to a pajama factory. In 1988, it was converted by Rodale Press into offices for its book division.

Laudenslager Grist, Feed, Grain and Coal building at 406 Minor St. in Emmaus looks like a combination barn and factory. The site is now occupied by Burkholder's Heating and Air Conditioning Co.

There were not many African Americans in the Lehigh Valley at the turn of the century. This rare photo of the Macungie baseball team taken between 1900-1905 shows young Robert Grant from Baltimore. His family worked in the home of Howard and Walter Singmaster.

The Macungie Iron Furnace was one of many that puffed smoke over the Lehigh Valley in the mid 19th century. When it was built in the 1870s, the local iron industry was going into a decline brought about by the collapse of the railroad building boom. The industry struggled into the 1890s, after which many iron furnaces were dismantled and sold for scrap.

The old-fashioned blacksmith shop was still a necessity of life in rural Lehigh County in the early 20th century. This picture shows the Macungie establishment of M. Rohrbach.

These smiling faces were part of St. Matthew's Evangelical Lutheran Sunday school class in Macungie. The photo was taken in 1900.

These three homes on Macungie's Main Street were considered upper-middle class when this picture was taken around 1900. Grace Lutheran Church, built in 1898, is at the end of the block.

Two young boys outside Schneckville's public school, circa 1910, eye a third who seems about to mount his bicycle. Note the fancy lamp on the front of the bike.

Upper Main St., Schnecksville, Pa.

Schnecksville was a prosperous farming community in 1910. This picture, taken from a postcard, shows homes on Upper Main Street.

In 1900, the public schoolhouse with bell tower (right) dominated the view on Schnecksville's Upper Main Street. Today the Villa Rosa Restaurant stands on the same site.

NORTHAMPTON

Northampton County, which takes its name from Northamptonshire, England, was created in 1752 by Thomas Penn, son of William Penn. He called the new area Northampton to honor his father-in-law, Lord Pomfret, a Northamptonshire land owner.

Penn gave the new county seat the name Easton after Lord Pomfret's manor house, Easton-Neston. A total of 10 counties would be formed out of the original Northampton, which, in those days, went as far north as the New York border.

The settlement of the Moravians in Bethlehem about 10 years before Easton's founding, created two distinct cultures in Northampton County's two largest towns. After the frontier-seeking Scots-Irish moved out of the county in the early 19th century, a Pennsylvania German culture developed, similar in some ways to that of Lehigh County.

Major changes that affected Northampton County in the late 19th century were the development of the iron industry, and more importantly, the cement industry.

In 1897, a number of investors including Allentown's Harry Trexler created the Lehigh Portland Cement Co. Its focal point was the town of Northampton which became a cement-making center.

By the 1920s, Northampton County was a center of both industry and agriculture.

Smith's Cash Grocer on Main Street in Bangor is shown decked out for the Old Home Week celebration in August 1914.

LEFT
William Martens operated
a wholesale liquor store on
Main Street in Bath
around 1920.

BELOW
Customers of A.J. Young's
General Merchandise
Store in Pen Argyl could
get their goods delivered in
this fancy wagon at the
turn of the century.

The staff of the Hanoverville Hotel pose for a picture in 1910.

The Sandts Eddy Hotel, operated by C. Holland, offered rest for early 20th century travelers who stopped at this Delaware River town.

James Siebert and Emily Zorn are shown under a big willow tree at Nazareth Hall. The date on the back of the photo is Aug. 20, 1885.

School students of Berlinsville, line up to have their photograph taken outside their school in 1920.

The congregation of Salem Church in Forks Township turned out to have a picture taken on Aug. 31, 1869.

The livery and boarding stable staff of Dr. A.H. Dorney at Siegfried, Northampton County, posed for this picture taken Oct. 18, 1899.

ABOVE
The cooper shop of Charles L. Cole was located outside of Kreidersville in 1907. A cooper was a barrel maker.

LEFT
This peaceful scene was photographed at the Zion Stone Church near Kreidersville on July 15, 1907. The men in front of the church (from left) are Daniel Weiss, P.B. Mack and E.B. Mack.

LEFT
The Leithsville Hotel was typical of the many country inns that took in guests in the late 19th century.

BELOW
This dirt road ran along the Delaware River at Sandts Eddy in 1920.

Roofing slate is piled up and ready for shipment at the Pen Argyl Slate Works in 1905.

Railroad tracks lead to the Pen Argyl Slate Works in this turn-of-the-century photo.

This picture of the slate works at Pen Argyl in 1910 shows that horsepower was used to pull the cables on the hoists to extract the slate.

This tractor is pulling a float for a parade in Nazareth about 1914. It represents the Lehigh & New England Railroad's repair shops at Pen Argyl.

The hotel at Treichlers greeted those crossing the Lehigh River on this bridge. The bridge was built as a toll structure in 1885 and was replaced in 1934 by a much larger span.

Workers for the Lehigh & New England Railroad, which served many area industries, are shown outside the Pen Argyl repair shops in 1910.

Slate workers in Pen Argyl in 1900 reflect the melting pot that is America.

The blacksmith shop was the garage of the 19th century. This shop is at Slateford, a small town on the Delaware River north of Portland in the 1880s.

This photo shows (from left) S.B. Weaver, Henry Cole and Daniel Weiss in Kreidersville in 1907. According to information on the back of the photo, Cole, who was born in 1817, was in excellent health.

The post office in Danielsville is shown sometime in the late 1920s.

Bauman's Sawmill at Siegfried's Bridge, now part of the Borough of Northampton, was one of many small industries that existed in Northampton County around 1900.

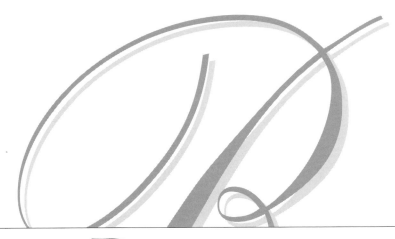

BUCKS

Bucks County takes its name from Buckinghamshire, England, and was one of the first three counties in Pennsylvania.

Founded in 1682, it was settled gradually in the late 17th and early 18th centuries. The early settlers were English, Scottish, Irish and German.

By the 1850s, Bucks County's rural character largely remained as it had been since its founding. The major change had been the introduction of the Delaware Canal in the 1830s that made that part of the county more populous. Although some industry did make use of the Delaware Canal, it never had the level of industrial development that blossomed on the Lehigh Canal.

The towns were farm market villages that showed little growth until the arrival of the railroads in the 1850s.

Quakertown offers a good example of this phenomenon. "In 1856, it comprised sixty-two dwellings, an increase of twenty-two in thirty-four years," says the 19th century Bucks County history. That same year the North Pennsylvania Railroad arrived. It was located about a mile from the old village of Quakertown.

Shortly thereafter, developers John Strawn and Joel B. Roberts laid out building lots around the railroad station. The settlement quickly took off and by 1867 had officially been recognized with a post office as the village of Richland Center.

The corporate limits of Quakertown were expanded in 1874, putting the new and old villages together under one municipal government.

In 1870, the Quakertown population was 863. In 1880, the combined population of Quakertown and Richland Center was 1,763, an increase of 900 people. By the dawn of the 20th century, Quakertown's industries produced everything from cigars to stoves.

ABOVE
This photo shows the interior of the boat, Molly-Polly Chunker, on a trip on the Lehigh and Delaware Canals conducted by Louis Comfort Tiffany, the man with the beard and hat. One of the women is Louisa Knox, daughter of the president of Lafayette College. Five months after the trip, Tiffany and Knox were married.

LEFT
Photographer Walter C. Tuckerman amuses children in Upper Black Eddy on a June afternoon in 1886. Tuckerman was part of a 12-person boat journey on the canals conducted by his friend, artist Louis Comfort Tiffany on the Molly-Polly Chunker. The boat was named for its motor power — the mules Molly and Polly and ultimate destination Mauch Chunk. The boat boasted carpeting, a dining room and two chefs.

Molly and Polly, with their driver, stop for a drink of Delaware Canal water.

LEFT

The life of a locktender's wife was not an easy one. Here the spouse of a locktender near Kintnersville cranks open the lock.

BELOW

Whatever other luxuries the Molly-Polly Chunker boasted, it did not have a laundry staff. But a locktender's wife was glad to make some extra money. Here, her family surrounds her at the washtub.

Residents along the canal at Kintnersville watch boat traffic in front of their home.

A group of children drift along the canal on a boat on a June afternoon in 1886.

ABOVE
Theresa Sine, standing, and her mother, Mary, pose on the front porch of their home on 3rd Street near Broad in Quakertown about 1917. Her parents started Sine's 5 & 10 in Quakertown, which is still owned and operated by the family.

LEFT
The Perkasie Volunteer Fire Company gathered for a summer picnic in 1900. The members hired musicians, (the four men at right). The company members are holding pretzels, beer and whiskey.

Juniper Street, Quakertown, Pa.

ABOVE
Hitching posts line the sidewalk in front of new stone houses on Juniper Street in Quakertown in 1907.

RIGHT
Workers in the molding room of Quakertown Stove Works on W. Broad Street between 3rd and 4th streets pose for this photograph in 1918.

Perkasie members of the Pennsylvania National Guard pose for a photograph in 1918 at their encampment on Tunnel Hill where they were posted to protect a train carrying steel from Bethlehem Steel Co. to Philadelphia during World War I.

MONTGOMERY

Montgomery County was founded in 1784. The origin of the name is unclear. Some sources claim it was named for Gen. Richard Montgomery, a Revolutionary War hero killed leading an assault on Quebec on Dec. 31, 1775. Others state it came from either William or Joseph Montgomery of Lancaster and Northumberland Counties, state legislators who sponsored the bill creating the county.

For most of its 19th century history, the county remained true to its rural roots. English, Welsh and Germans were the predominant ethnic groups. "In 1880 the county consisted of rural townships with a few river boroughs strung along the Schuylkill and a few others along the railroads," notes the 1983 county history. Norristown and Pottstown were among those boroughs with an industrial base.

Souderton, called Souder's Lumberyard on an 1849 map, was another place that owed its growth to the railroads.

The borough of Telford, split between Bucks and Montgomery counties, offers a good example of the development of a Montgomery County community. It began life in 1840 and first appeared on maps that year as the site of "Hendrick's Blacksmith Shop." Later the area became known as County Line after the County Line Hotel.

In 1880, when the village applied for incorporation as a borough it was denied because a state law forbid any town that was in two counties to be incorporated.

In 1886, the Bucks County section was granted a charter by the county court and took the name Telford. In 1897 the Montgomery County section was granted a charter by its county court under the name West Telford. They were not finally united until 1937.

A hot-air balloon ascension was always a crowd-pleaser in the late 19th and early 20th centuries. This event in Pottstown, sponsored perhaps by the local Shriners chapter, attracted a number of young boys.

The Oak Grocery Store at E. Broad Street in Souderton provided its turn-of-the-century customers with a variety of goods. The building's handsome mansard roof adds a touch of 19th-century style.

The open road is W. Broad Street in Souderton and this is the community's first automobile. Is that wagon driver at right thinking "Get a horse?"

A 1907 picnic excursion to an amusement park at Ringing Rocks in Pottsgrove Township turned out to be more than its participants bargained for when a trolley derailed. No one was hurt, but a crowd gathered quickly.

Elaborate decorations and a parade, sometime around the turn of the century, fill downtown Pottstown, perhaps for a July 4 celebration.

ABOVE
Posters on easels promoting the latest films are propped against the Palace Theater (building at right) on 4th Street in East Greenville. The theater was built in 1910, abandoned in 1914 and demolished in 1936.

LEFT
Pictured on this postcard is the Old Depot where railroad tracks cross Route 113 in Souderton.

ABOVE

The Keely House at the corner of Main and Bank streets in East Greenville about 1890 was a busy place. It is now the Owl's Home.

LEFT

The Perkiomen Inn at Schwenksville was one of many hotels that catered to the trainloads of summer visitors who came to the region between 1869 and 1920 to enjoy the nearby amusement park or to boat and swim in the Perkiomen Creek. The hotel was built in 1895 by Mr. and Mrs. Morris Carl, who operated it until 1919.

ABOVE
The Abram Cox Stove Co. that opened in Lansdale in 1887 was one of the leading retail stores of the town. This photo shows the members of the polishing and plating department on a patriotic float for some holiday.

LEFT
The Hallowell Fire Department had handsome horses and a rough-and-ready crew like many small rural fire stations at the turn of the century.

CARBON

Carbon County and anthracite coal have been synonymous for over 200 years. It was in 1791 that a hunter named Philip Ginter, looking for game to feed his family, slipped on something. In the fading twilight he saw a hard, shiny rock with a black surface he knew was coal.

From Ginter's accidental discovery sprang an industrial empire. By the 1850s, the Lehigh Canal, thanks to its builders Josiah White, Eriskine Hazard and a lot of largely unknown German, Irish and African-American shovel-wielding canal diggers, was sending anthracite coal to the homes and factories of the eastern United States. Later, railroads would displace the canal boats as carriers of the black diamonds.

Fortunes were made from anthracite in the 19th century and not just by mine owners. Lehigh Valley Railroad founder Asa Packer and his family built summer mansions in the county seat of Mauch Chunk, now Jim Thorpe, testifying to the wealth of the owners.

But King Coal's reign was not a peaceful one. The dangers of mining and demands of mine owners, coupled with ethnic prejudice, often created tensions that spilled over into violence.

In the 1870s, a group of Irish miners, saloon owners and Democratic politicians, labeled the Mollie Maguires, became the focal point of trials that attracted worldwide attention to Carbon County and its neighbor, Schuylkill County. Although the leadership of the so-called Mollies were executed, the movement for a miner's union remained strong through the late 19th and early 20th centuries.

Starting in 1872, Coalport, one mile from East Mauch Chunk, was the main transfer and loading point for coal from the Lehigh Canal. This photo shows a canal boat about to enter the Coalport lock.

ABOVE
The Lehigh Valley Railroad's shops at Packerton, outside of Lehighton, are shown here in 1900. It was here that railroad cars and engines were repaired.

LEFT
In the late 19th and early 20th centuries, there were few more popular spots for a summer vacation than the cool mountain region of Glen Onoko and its waterfalls. The Hotel Wahnetah, shown here in 1907, was one of the resort hotels built in that area.

The Ziegenfuss
Boat Yard and store
at Rickertsville,
also known as
North Weissport,
was near Lock 8 on
the Lehigh Canal.

Oak Grove
Seminary in
Weatherly is visible
on the hill in the
background. In the
foreground, the
Gilbert House
Hotel can be seen
in this 1880 photo.
Crossing guards
monitored the
intersection from
the house in the
lower left.

358. Penn Haven Jct. Looking West. 5-17-12.

ABOVE

The Penn Haven Junction of the Lehigh Valley Railroad was about six miles south of Weatherly on a line that extended between Buffalo and Newark. There was a restaurant in the house behind the station in this 1912 photo.

RIGHT

A horse and wagon are used to pick up freight at the Central Railroad of New Jersey station in Lehighton around 1900. Houses visible are on 1st Street in the background.

LEFT
The Weigh Lock on the Lehigh Canal at Mauch Chunk was installed in 1913. The canal boat was placed in the lock chamber. As the water was let out, the boat came to rest on a cradle on a large scale that would weigh a boat's cargo.

BELOW
Around the turn of the century, Palmerton got its first public mode of transportation.

In the early morning hours of Dec. 15, 1901, a flash flood combined with melting mountain snow swept down the Lehigh River and hit Mauch Chunk. The flood damaged the Central Railroad of New Jersey at Mauch Chunk, now Jim Thorpe. St. Mark's Church is in the background.

This photo, taken on Dec. 18, 1901, shows flood-ravaged tracks near the Central of New Jersey Railroad station. Central officials estimated damage to the line at $500,000. Workers repaired the damage to the rails, but a flood in February 1902 washed out the area again.

LEFT

A car travels on the Mauch Chunk Switchback Gravity Railroad to give tourists a thrill ride, on the Mount Jefferson Plane near Summit Hill around the turn of the century. The length of track was 2,070 feet and the incline was 462 feet.

ABOVE

When this picture was taken in the late 1870s, the Mauch Chunk Switchback Railroad had evolved from a coal-hauling operation to a tourist thrill ride up Mount Pisgah. This photo shows two cables riding over steel drums. The cables, hauled by a steam engine, pulled a passenger car uphill. By 1900, 10,000 people a day were taking excursions on the switchback.

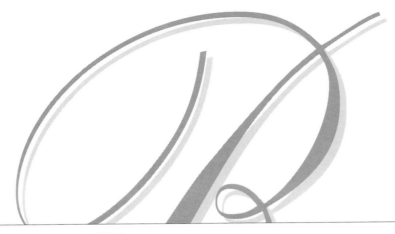

BERKS

Founded in 1752, Berks County takes its name from Berkshire County in England. For most of its history, Berks was a center of agriculture. The county seat, Reading, was named for Reading, England. Most of the population was Pennsylvania German.

Reading was a market town where farmers went to sell their produce and to buy items they did not make for themselves. Market days and fair days would find the town crowded.

"Dancing, drinking and fighting were conspicuous features," notes the 1909 History of Berks County. The same combination of canals and railroads that opened up other counties took place in Berks. The Philadelphia & Reading Railroad arrived in the 1830s and soon became a major employer and powerful force in the community. Reading also was the center of hundreds of industries. For example, the modern American automobile industry was born in Berks County, thanks to a large number of skilled wagon and bicycle makers who were located there.

Kutztown, founded in 1779 and incorporated in 1815, takes its name from its founder George Kutz. In 1866, the Keystone State Normal School, a state training school for teachers, opened there. In 1928, it was renamed Kutztown.

The Kutztown Post Office at Main and Greenwich streets was a handsome Victorian structure with a Queen Anne turret. This photograph shows it decorated for a patriotic turn-of-the-century holiday.

A sign above the bar at the Douglassville Hotel in Berks County says, "No drinks sold to minors," but children were admitted, at least for this photograph. According to information on the back of the photo, those shown include Walter Shirey, Uncle Daniel Shirey, Rhia Shirey and Aunt Mame.

This Kutztown general store offered a wide variety of items ranging from coffee to boys' shirts at the turn of the century.

These young members of the Oley baseball team show that they did not need fancy uniforms to form a team in the 1920s.

The 1898 football team of Keystone Normal School, now Kutztown University.

This Berks County farm family had its picture taken sometime in the 1800s, possibly at a family reunion. Their faces and hands suggest lives of hard work.

The Leesport Union Church, also called St. John's Church, Reformed and Lutheran, was founded in the mid 18th century. The hill on which it stands is very commanding, making the church a prominent object for many miles, according to an 1886 county history. This picture was taken in November 1906.